Snickers

Sally Odgers

Illustrated by Annie White

Snickers was a duck, a fine white duck.
He belonged to Mei Ling.
"A duck is a funny sort of pet, Mei Ling,"
said Annabelle.
"Why?" said Mei Ling. "Why is a duck a funny sort of pet?"

Annabelle laughed.

"I like dogs.

You can hug a dog. You can't hug a duck."

"I can hug Snickers," said Mei Ling.

Mei Ling picked up Snickers and gave him a hug.
Snickers had a long white neck
and a big yellow bill.
He twisted his long white neck.
He tucked his big yellow bill under Mei Ling's chin.
"See? He isn't a funny sort of pet," said Mei Ling.

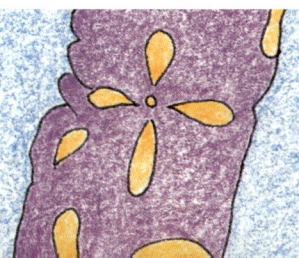

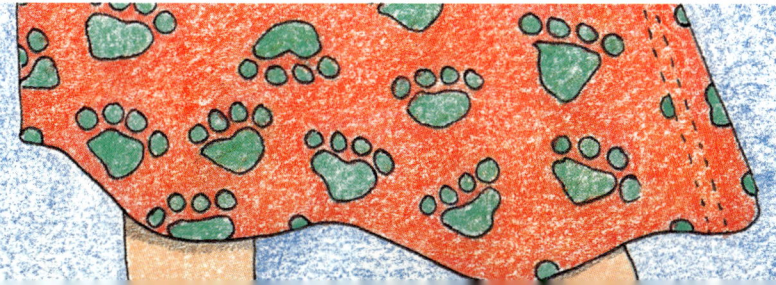

Annabelle laughed. "I like dogs. You can take a dog for a walk. You cannot take a duck for a walk."

"I can take Snickers for a walk," said Mei Ling. "Come on, Snickers."

Waddle-waddle. Waddle-waddle.
Snickers had big flat feet and a short white tail.
The big flat feet waddled very fast.
The short white tail wagged back and forth.
"See? He isn't a funny sort of pet," said Mei Ling.

Annabelle laughed. "I like dogs.
You can give a dog a bath.
You cannot give a duck a bath."
"I can give Snickers a bath," said Mei Ling.
Mei Ling carried him to the pond.

Paddle-paddle. Paddle-paddle.
Snickers had big flat feet and big white wings.
The big flat feet paddled him through the water.
The big white wings flapped and splashed until
Snickers was quite clean.
"See? He isn't a funny sort of pet," said Mei Ling.

Annabelle laughed. "I like dogs.
You can teach a dog to do tricks.
You cannot teach a duck to do tricks."
"No," said Mei Ling.
"You cannot teach a duck to do tricks.
I guess he is a funny sort of pet."

Just then, Snickers turned upside down.
His big feet paddled and his short white tail stuck up out of the water.
His big yellow bill scooped up a tasty plant.
"He is doing a trick," cried Annabelle.

"That isn't a trick," said Mei Ling.
"That is how Snickers finds food."
"He is funny," said Annabelle.
"He is a funny pet. I like you, Snickers."

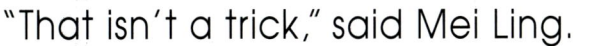

"I thought you liked dogs," said Mei Ling.

"I do," said Annabelle. "I do like dogs. But now I like ducks, too."

Mei Ling smiled.

Annabelle smiled.

Mei Ling and Annabelle walked home. Snickers waddled behind them.